BEGINNING
WORSHIP KEYBOARD

INSTRUCTION FOR
THE WORSHIP MUSICIAN

SANDY HOFFMAN

Emerald
Books

P.O. Box 635
Lynnwood, WA 98046

Emerald Books are distributed through YWAM Publishing. For a full list of titles, including other worship resources, visit our website at:

www.ywampublishing.com

Published by Emerald Books
P.O. Box 635
Lynnwood, Washington 98046

ISBN: 1-883002-92-3

Beginning Worship Keyboard

Printed in the United States of America.

DEDICATION

To my brother, K. Marc Hoffman, whose
help and attention to detail made this
project both a possibility and a pleasure.

OTHER TITLES BY SANDY HOFFMAN

Beginning (Level 1):
Beginning Worship Guitar (book)   ISBN: 1-883002-72-9
Beginning Worship Guitar (instructional video) ISBN: 1-883002-76-1

Intermediate (Level 2):
Essential Worship Guitar (book)   ISBN: 1-883002-73-7
Essential Worship Guitar (instructional video) ISBN: 1-883002-75-3

CONTENTS

IN CLOSING

INTRODUCTION

Much of today's worship music is written from a guitarist's point of view. Whether you've had years of experience on the keyboard or you're just learning where the on/off switch is located, you may need a radical new approach to your instrument. Why not learn worship keyboard from a fresh perspective?

Beginning Worship Keyboard is designed to put the aspiring worship keyboardist on the same page with a worship community that often seems so guitar oriented. This book offers an easy-to-understand approach to the art of keyboard accompaniment.

Beginning Worship Keyboard is laid out in seven sections which build in a logical progression from just getting started to playing songs all together. Along the way the keyboardist is exposed to contemporary worship chord diagrams, arpeggios and pads, rhythmic variations, major and minor keys, the number system, and time signatures. Also included are appendix items such as tuning the band and the number system.

As you move prayerfully through *Beginning Worship Keyboard*, it is my hope and desire that you'll become fully equipped and deeply inspired to lift up praises just as David did.

Let the peoples praise You, O God. Let all the peoples praise You!
                                                            Psalm 67:3

Have fun!

Yours in Christ,

Sandy

I. GETTING STARTED

ABOUT THE KEYBOARD

I.   **The keyboard is most commonly an instrument of 88 keys.**

The keys of the keyboard are named **C - C# (C sharp) - D - D# - E - F - F# - G - G# - A - A# - B**. The sharped notes can also be identified by their "flat" names. This is known as "enharmonic" spelling.
C# (C sharp) = D♭ (D flat).

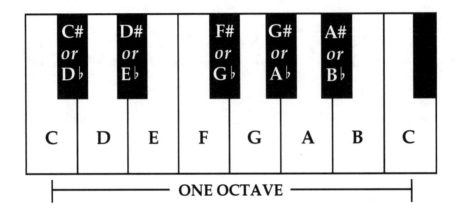

Notes are repeated from left to right up the keyboard in groups of twelve notes. They progress in "octaves" from the lowest to the highest and total eighty-eight.

II.   **The keys of the keyboard can be played as chords, arpeggios, or pads.**

A *chord* is three or more notes played at the same time.

Arpeggios are "broken chords." Chords are broken by playing the notes of the chord one at a time (see page 39).

Pads are often played on the electronic keyboard. These notes or chords are held for longer numbers of beats and mimic the sounds of stringed instruments, string orchestras, electronic organs, and other legato instruments (see page 49).

PLAYING THE KEYBOARD

I.   **"MIDDLE C" INDICATOR—** `M` `C`

Throughout *Beginning Worship Keyboard*, the middle C indicator will provide a "bench mark" or starting point for each new chord. Middle C is located roughly in the center of the eighty-eight key keyboard. *(Count up forty white and black keys from the lowest left hand note.)*

Locate the middle C indicator on each chord diagram before building the chord. This will help to maintain consistent chord positioning. The *regular reference to middle C* in each chord diagram makes it easy to identify the specific location of *any* chord on the keyboard.

II.   **It is vitally important for the keyboardist to establish good posture habits from the very beginning.**

To increase endurance during playing, the back should remain straight at all times.

Be sure to sit when playing for longer periods. Using the sustain pedal on the electronic keyboard while standing can cause back problems in no time!

III. **The correct hand position is also imperative for the keyboardist.**

The player's hand should look as if it is holding a tennis ball. The palm is down with the back of the hand remaining parallel (flat) to the keys at all times. Keep the elbows relaxed and hanging comfortably next to the body. Strike the keys with the finger tips.

Remember: correct hand position greatly reduces fatigue.

ABOUT CHORD CONSTRUCTION

I.   **A chord is a combination of three or more notes played at the same time** (see page 10).

The notes in the C major scale are: C, D, E, F, G, A, & B. Chords in the key of C are constructed with combinations of these notes. To make the C major triad (three notes), simply play the 1st, 3rd, and 5th notes of the C major scale at the same time (C, E, G).

II.   **Notes in a chord may be repeated within the chord.**

The C major triad is spelled C, E, G, but these notes may be doubled within the chord by using the left and right hands.

Think:

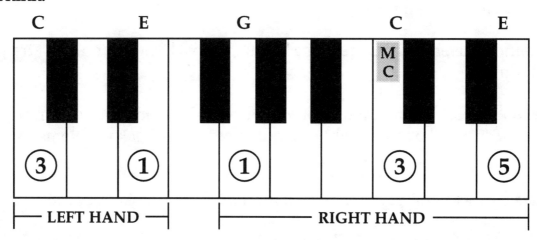

III.   **Notes moved to the right one half-step to the next highest note are considered to be "sharp" (#)** (see Appendix II).

IV.   **Notes moved one half-step to the next lowest key are considered to be "flat" (♭)** (see Appendix II).

ABOUT CHORD DIAGRAMS

I. CHORD DIAGRAMS

By using chord diagrams, the keyboardist is able to understand where to place the left- and right-hand fingers to form a particular chord.

THE C MAJOR TRIAD CHORD DIAGRAM

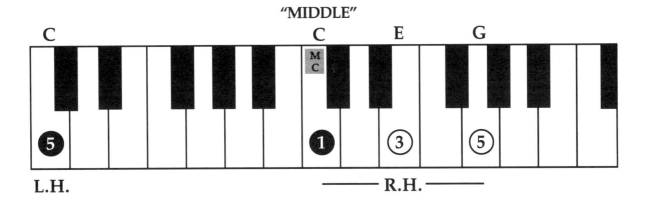

II. NOTE NAMES—C, E, G

The letter name of each note to be played in a specific chord will appear over the corresponding key in the chord diagram.

It is vital that the student begin to recognize *and* memorize the names of the twelve notes which are repeated from left to right along the keyboard. (C - C# - D - D# - E - F - F# - G - G# - A - A# - B)

III. FINGER POSITION MARKERS—③

The circles placed on the keys in the chord diagram are finger position markers. These tell where to place the left- or right-hand finger tips for any given chord.

IV.   FINGER NUMBERS—1, 2, 3, 4, 5

The left- and right-hand fingers of the keyboardist are numbered:

1 (thumb), 2 (index), 3 (middle), 4 (ring), and 5 (pinky).

The **C Major** chord diagram indicates the following:

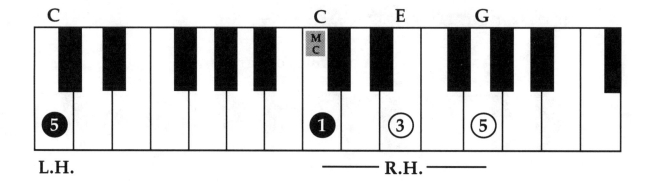

L.H.   —— R.H. ——

1. Place the first right-hand (R.H.) finger (thumb) on middle C.
2. Place the third right-hand (R.H.) finger (middle) on the note E.
3. Place the fifth right-hand (R.H.) finger (pinky) on the note G.
4. Place the fifth left-hand (L.H.) finger (pinky) on the note C one octave below middle C.

V.   BASS (ROOT) NOTE INDICATORS— **①**

The black circle placed on the keys in the chord diagram indicates the position of the "bass" or "root" note. This is the lowest note of the chord and has the same letter name as the chord. Therefore, the root or bass note of the C major triad is C.

The **bass note** of a chord is often played with a right-hand finger and also **doubled** with the left hand in a lower octave. This repetition of the bass note in the lower octave reinforces the foundation of the chord and adds strength to the voicing.

ABOUT INVERSIONS

I.   In order to create chord voicings which are pleasing to the ear and easy to reach with the fingers, chords are often "inverted." *Inverted chords are constructed by rearranging the order of the notes in the chord.* In Beginning Worship Keyboard we will learn chord voicings known as right-hand inversions.

II.   With chord inversions the note *positions* are movable but the *names* of the notes within the chord remain the same.

        Root position of the C Major triad: C, E, G

        First inversion of the C Major triad: E, G, **C**

        Second inversion of the C Major triad: G, **C**, E

III.   The C Major triad and right-hand inversions:

The C Major triad is spelled **C**, E, G. This is known as "root position." In this form the bass or lowest note of the chord is the note **C**.

ROOT POSITION

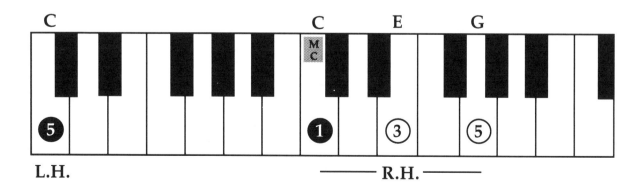

L.H.   —— R.H. ——

RIGHT-HAND FIRST INVERSION

To construct a **right-hand first inversion** of the C Major triad, we begin with the note E (two whole steps above the root) and spell the chord E, G, **C**. The lowest right-hand note has now become the highest. *Continue to play the note C with the left hand.

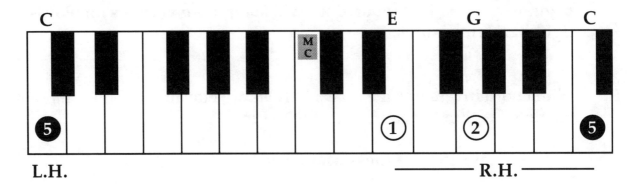

RIGHT-HAND SECOND INVERSION

To construct a **right-hand second inversion** of the C Major triad, we begin with the note G (three and one-half steps above the root) and spell the chord G, **C**, E. Again the lowest right-hand note has been relocated to the highest position. The left hand will continue to play the note C.

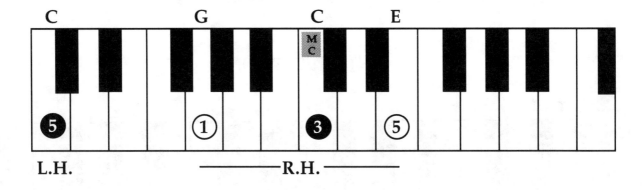

*In a "true inversion," the left-hand root note doubles the lowest note in the right hand. For ease of chord voicing, only right-hand inversions will be used throughout the Beginning Worship Keyboard book.

II. THE KEY OF C MAJOR

CHORD DIAGRAM REVIEW

C MAJOR TRIAD CHORD DIAGRAM

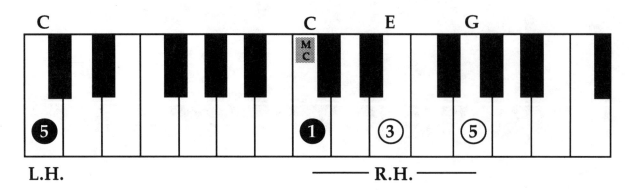

M C (gray box)	= MIDDLE C INDICATOR
C E G	= NAME OF NOTE INDICATORS
1 **5** (filled circles)	= BASS OR ROOT NOTE INDICATOR (played with the *first finger* of the right hand and also an octave[1], or eight notes, lower with the *fifth finger* of the left hand)
③ ⑤ (open circles)	= FINGER POSITION MARKERS
L.H. or R.H.	= LEFT HAND OR RIGHT HAND

---

[1] See page 14, ABOUT CHORD DIAGRAMS

CHORDS IN THE KEY OF C

Key of C **CHORD NAME**:	C	Dm	Em	**F**	**G**	Am	Bdim	**C**
SCALE DEGREE NUMBER[1] :	**I**	ii	iii	**IV**	**V**	vi	vii	**I**

C Major—root position[2] (built upon scale degree I)

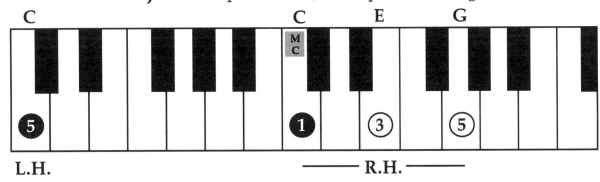

F Major—second inversion (built upon scale degree IV)

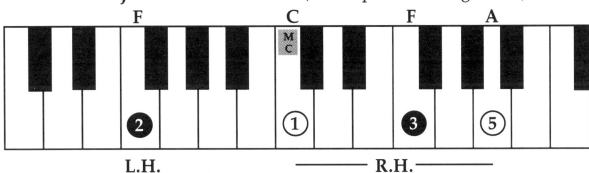

G Major—first inversion (built upon scale degree V)

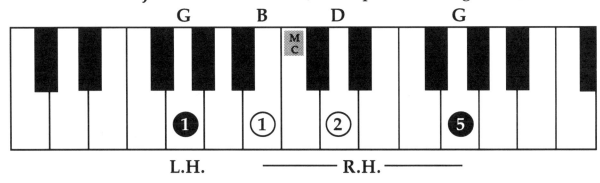

---

[1] See page 76, APPENDIX I, THE NUMBER SYSTEM
[2] See pages 15 and 16, ABOUT INVERSIONS

ABOUT PLAYING CHORDS

I. A keyboardist plays "rhythm keyboard" by "chording."

II. Chording is accomplished by playing all the notes in a chord at the same time.

III. Rhythm keyboard parts are often communicated with simple diagonal lines: / / / /.

Each line represents one beat.   / / / /
1 2 3 4

IV. For each diagonal line (/) play the chord one time.

ABOUT THE TIME SIGNATURE

I. The top number of the *time signature* determines the number of beats to be played per measure of music. The bottom number indicates the type of note receiving one beat.

$\frac{4}{4}$ = four beats per measure
= a "quarter note" ($\downarrow$ or /) receives one beat

For each measure count steadily and chord: **one, two, three, four**.

$\frac{4}{4}$ / / / /   / / / /   / / / /   / / / /
1 2 3 4   1 2 3 4   1 2 3 4   1 2 3 4

$\frac{3}{4}$ = three beats per measure
= a quarter note ($\downarrow$ or /) receives one beat

For each measure count steadily and chord: **one, two, three**.

$\frac{3}{4}$ / / /   / / /   / / /   / / /
1 2 3   1 2 3   1 2 3   1 2 3

THE C MAJOR CHORD

C Major (root position)

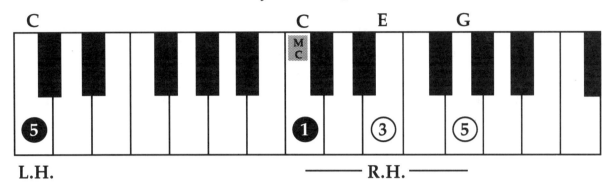

Play C Major, chording steadily one, two, three, four with the *right hand*.

With the *fifth finger* (pinky) of the *left hand* play the root or bass note (**C**) one octave below middle C. Do this on the first beat of each new measure.

$\frac{4}{4}$ C   C   C   C
 / / / /   / / / /   / / / /   / / / /
1 2 3 4

Play C Major, chording steadily one, two, three.

Continue to play the bass note of the C chord on the first beat of each new measure.

$\frac{3}{4}$ C   C   C   C
 / / /   / / /   / / /   / / /
1 2 3

THE F MAJOR CHORD

F Major (second inversion)

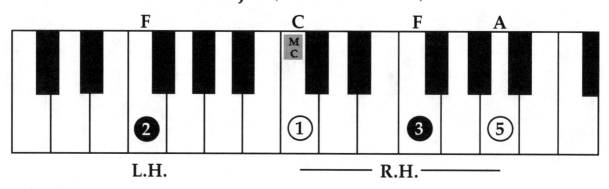

L.H. ————— R.H. —————

Play F Major, chording steadily one, two, three, four with the *right hand*.

With the *second finger* (index) of the *left hand* play the root or bass note (**F**) in the octave below middle C. Do this on the first beat of each new measure.

$\frac{4}{4}$ F   F   F   F

/ / / /   / / / /   / / / /   / / / /

Play F Major, chording steadily one, two, three.

$\frac{3}{4}$ F   F   F   F

/ / /   / / /   / / /   / / /

C and F chords—one, two, three, four

$\frac{4}{4}$ C   F   C   F

/ / / /   / / / /   / / / /   / / / /

THE G MAJOR CHORD

G **Major** (first inversion)

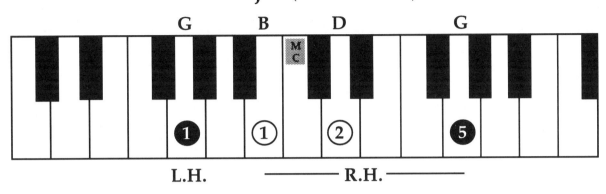

G Major—one, two, three, four

With the *first finger* (thumb) of the *left hand* play the root or bass note (**G**) in the octave below middle C. Do this on the first beat of each new measure.

$\frac{4}{4}$ G   / / / /   G   / / / /   G   / / / /   G   / / / /

G Major—one, two, three

$\frac{3}{4}$ G   / / /   G   / / /   G   / / /   G   / / /

C, F, and G Major chords

$\frac{4}{4}$ C   / / / /   F   / / / /   G   / / / /   C   / / / /

EXERCISE 1—Chording the Keys

Play, chording steadily one, two, three, four.

♩ = 84 (a tempo marking which indicates to play at 84 beats per minute—see APPENDIX IV)

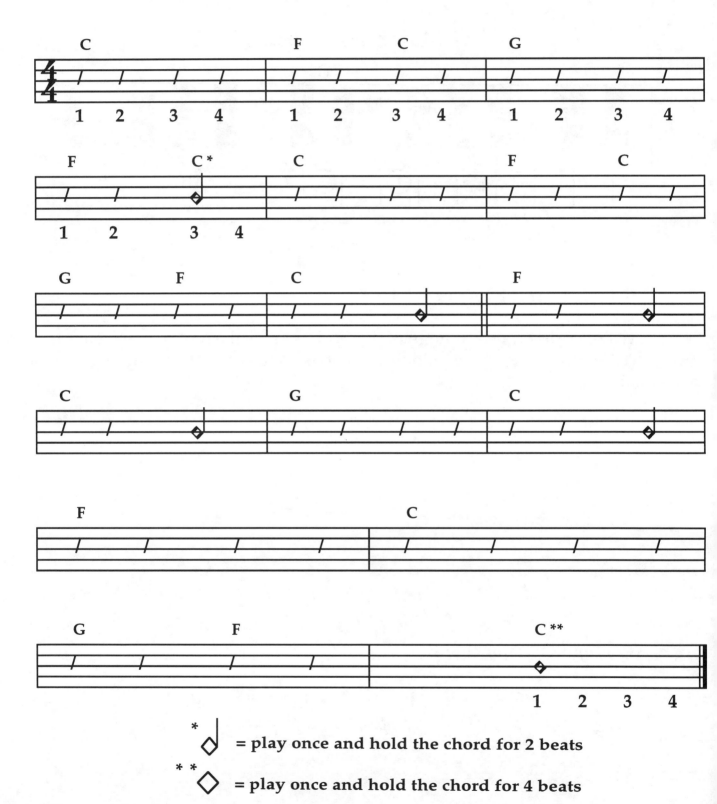

* ♩◇ = play once and hold the chord for 2 beats

** ◇ = play once and hold the chord for 4 beats

EXERCISE 2—Chording in 3/4 Time

Play, chording steadily one, two, three.

♩ = 100 (a tempo marking which indicates to play at 100 beats per minute—see APPENDIX IV)

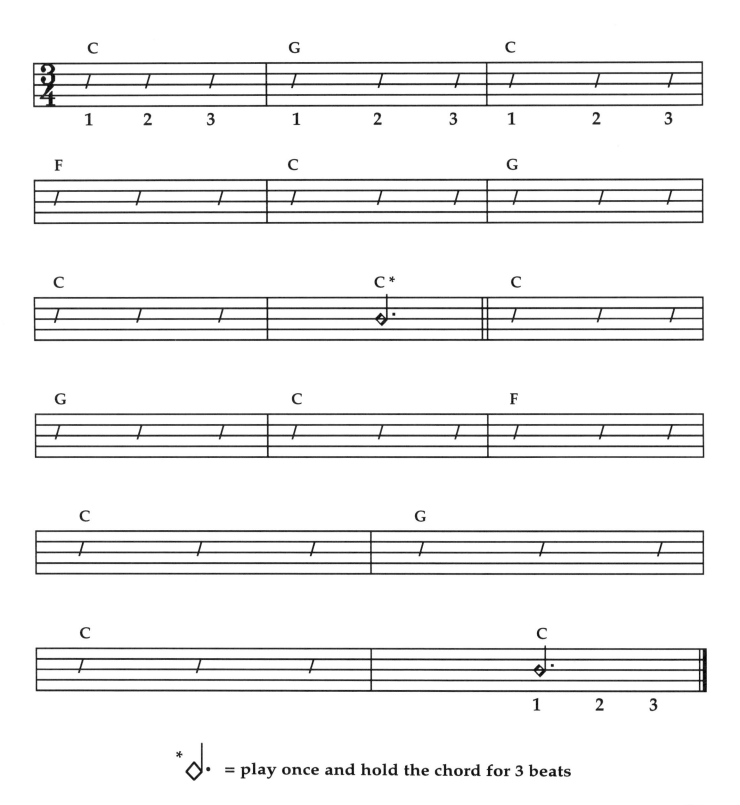

*♩• = play once and hold the chord for 3 beats

THEY'RE FOR YOU—Key of C

Play, chording steadily one, two, three, four.

♩ = 76

Sandy Hoffman

III. THE KEY OF G MAJOR

ABOUT COLOR CHORDS

I.   **"2(no3)" chords and "sus" chords (suspensions) are also known as "color chords." As such they are valuable substitutes for major triads.**

Color chords are pleasing to the ear and are often used to create a worshipful atmosphere.

II.   **The 2(no3) chord is constructed by lowering the note which is the 3rd in the major triad one whole step.**

The C Major triad is spelled C, E, G. By lowering the 3rd (E) one whole step we change the spelling to C, <u>D</u>, G. This causes the C chord to become the C2(no3) chord (see page 29).

III.   **The sus or "sus4" chord is constructed by raising the note which is the 3rd in the major triad one half-step.**

The D Major triad is spelled D, F#, A. By raising the 3rd (F#) one half-step we change the spelling to D, <u>G</u>, A. This causes the D chord to become the Dsus or Dsus4 chord (see page 29).

CHORDS IN THE KEY OF G

Key of G **CHORD NAME**:	G	A m	Bm	**C**	**D**	Em	F#dim	**G**
SCALE DEGREE NUMBER:	**I**	ii	iii	**IV**	**V**	vi	vii	**I**

G Major–root position (built upon scale degree **I**)

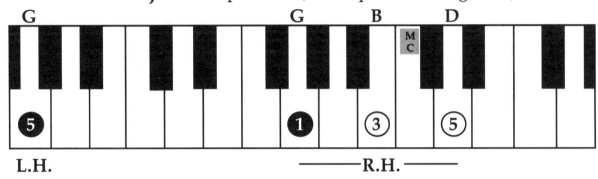

C2(no3)[1]–second inversion (built upon scale degree **IV**)

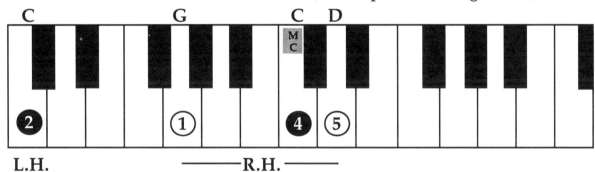

Dsus–first inversion (built upon scale degree **V**)

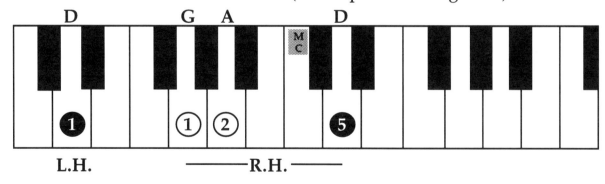

---

[1] See page 28, ABOUT COLOR CHORDS

THE G MAJOR CHORD

G Major (root position)

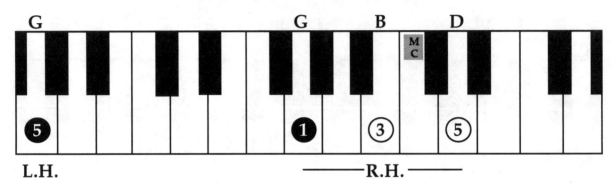

Play G Major, chording steadily one, two, three, four with the *right hand*.

With the *fifth finger* of the *left hand* play the root or bass note (**G**) in the second octave below middle C. Do this on the first beat of each new measure.

$\frac{4}{4}$ G / / / /   G / / / /   G / / / /   G / / / /

Play G Major, chording steadily, one, two, three.

Continue to play the bass note of the G Major chord on the first beat of each new measure.

$\frac{3}{4}$ G / / /   G / / /   G / / /   G / / /

THE C2(no3) CHORD

C2(no3) (second inversion)

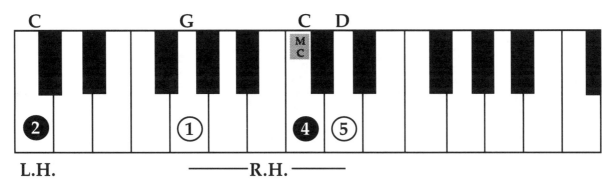

C2(no3) chord—one, two, three, four

With the *second finger* of the *left hand* play the bass note (**C**) one octave below middle C. Do this on the first beat of each new measure.

$\frac{4}{4}$ **C2(no3)**
/ / / /   / / / /   / / / /   / / / /

C2(no3) chord—one, two, three

$\frac{3}{4}$ **C2(no3)**
/ / /   / / /   / / /   / / /

G and C2(no3) chords—one, two, three, four

$\frac{4}{4}$ **G**   **C2(no3)**   **G**   **C2(no3)**
/ / / /   / / / /   / / / /   / / / / :||

(repeat the line)

THE Dsus CHORD

Dsus (first inversion)

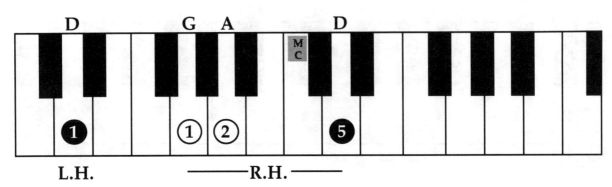

Dsus chord

With the *first finger* of the *left hand* play the bass note (**D**) in the octave below middle C. Do this on the first beat of each new measure.

$\frac{4}{4}$ **Dsus**
/ / / /   / / / /   / / / /   / / / /

Dsus chord

$\frac{3}{4}$ **Dsus**
/ / /   / / /   / / /   / / /

G, C2(no3), and Dsus chords

$\frac{4}{4}$ **G**   **C2(no3)**   **Dsus**   **C2(no3)**
/ / / /   / / / /   / / / /   / / / / :‖

(repeat the line)

EXERCISE 3

Play, chording steadily one, two, three, four.

♩ = 84

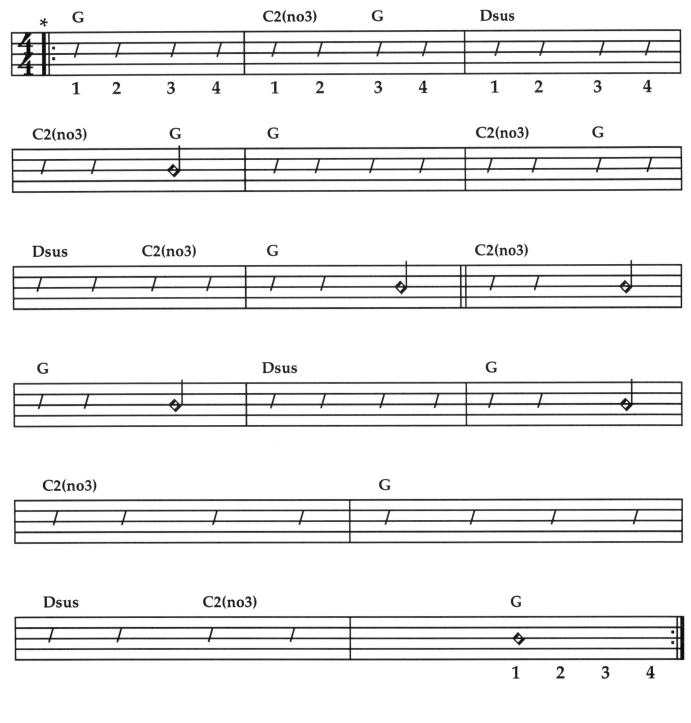

EXERCISE 4

Play, chording steadily one, two, three.

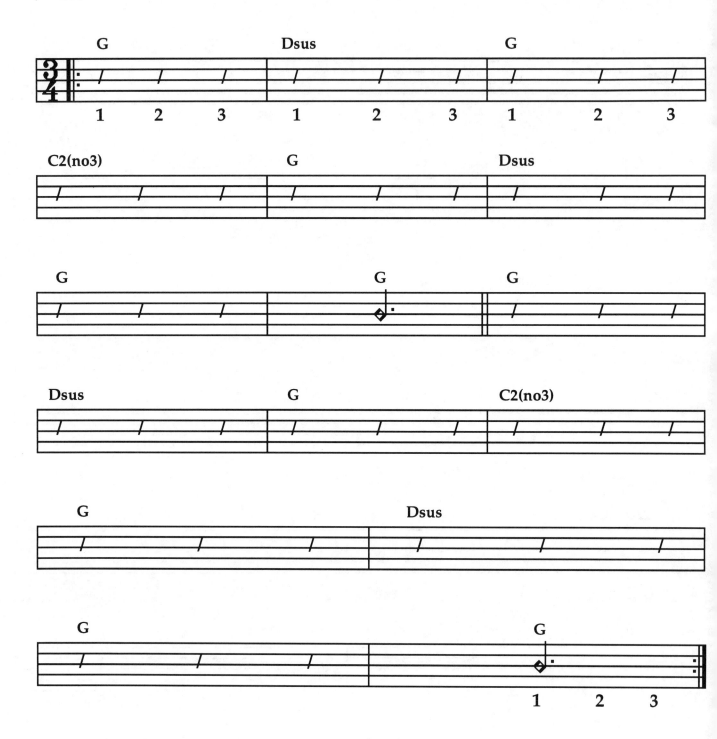

ABOUT RESTS

I.   For each note used in music there is a corresponding rest. A rest is a period of silence. The length of the silence depends upon the type of rest used.

II. The following are values of common notes and rests:

	Note:	Rest:	Value:
whole	o	—	4 beats
half	♩	▬	2 beats
dotted half	♩.	▬:	3 beats
quarter	♩	𝄽	1 beat
dotted quarter	♩.	𝄽.	1 1/2 beats
eighth	♪	⁊	1/2 beat (each)

III. While playing "I Give You Everything" on the following page, the keyboardist should continue to chord steadily over the notes, rests, and lyrics unless otherwise indicated.

I GIVE YOU EVERYTHING

Sandy Hoffman

*A rest is a period of silence (see page 35, ABOUT RESTS)

IV. THE KEY OF D MAJOR

CHORDS IN THE KEY OF D

Key of D **CHORD NAME:**	**D**	Em	F#m	**G**	**A**	Bm	C#dim	**D**
SCALE DEGREE NUMBER:	**I**	ii	iii	**IV**	**V**	vi	vii	**I**

D Major–root position (built upon scale degree I)

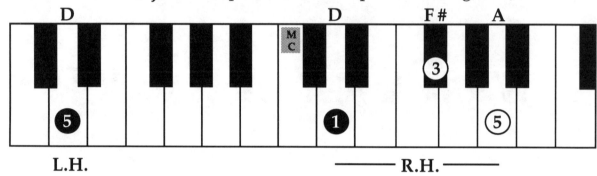

G Major-second inversion (built upon scale degree IV)

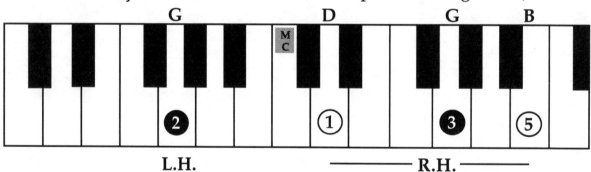

A Major–first inversion (built upon scale degree V)

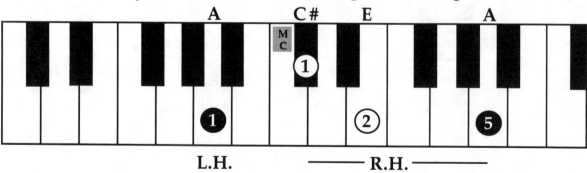

ABOUT ARPEGGIOS

I.   *Arpeggios* are broken chords. Chords are broken when the notes of the chord are played one at a time.

II. Playing arpeggios provides a more ornamental way of presenting chords. Arpeggios create movement in chord accompaniments and make them even more interesting to the listener.

III. To arpeggiate chords, play one note of the chord for each diagonal line (or beat) of the measure. *This is called a quarter note rhythm pattern.*

To arpeggiate the D Major chord[1], play the right hand as follows:

NOTE:	D F# A F#	D F# A F#	D F# A F#	D F# A F#
	/ / / /	/ / / /	/ / / /	/ / / /
BEAT:	1 2 3 4	1 2 3 4	1 2 3 4	1 2 3 4

IV. The keyboardist may also play *two notes of the chord* for each diagonal line (or beat) of the measure. *This is called an eighth note rhythm pattern.*

NOTE:	D F# A F# D F# A F#	D F# A F# D F# A F#
	/ + / + / + / +	/ + / + / + / +
BEAT:	1 and 2 and 3 and 4 and	1 and 2 and 3 and 4 and

V.   Remember to play the bass note of the D Major chord (D) with the fifth finger of the left hand on the first beat of each new measure.

---

[1] See page 38, CHORDS IN THE KEY OF D

THE D MAJOR CHORD

D Major (root position)

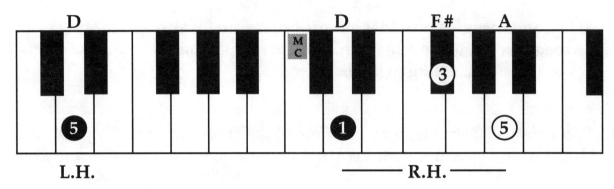

Play D Major in arpeggio style–D, F#, A, F#–one note of the chord for each diagonal line (or beat) of the measure.

With the *fifth finger* of the *left hand* play the bass note (**D**) in the octave below middle C.

$\frac{4}{4}$ **D**   **D**   **D**   **D**

/ / / /   / / / /   / / / /   / / / /

D F# A F#

Play D Major steadily in arpeggio style—one, two, three.

Note the time signature. There are only three beats per measure. This means the chord is played D, F#, A over and over.

$\frac{3}{4}$ **D**   **D**   **D**   **D**

/ / /   / / /   / / /   / / /

D F# A

THE G MAJOR CHORD

G Major (second inversion)

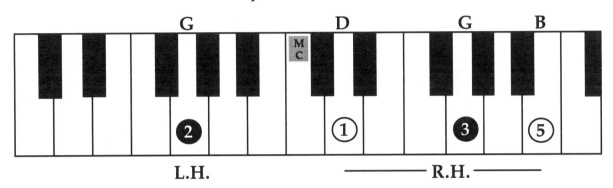

L.H. ————— R.H. —————

Play G Major in arpeggio style–D, G, B, G–one note of the chord for each diagonal line (or beat) of the measure.

With the *second finger* of the *left hand* play the bass note (**G**) in the octave below middle C.

$\frac{4}{4}$ **G**

/ / / /   / / / /   / / / /   / / / /

D G B G

Play G and D in arpeggio style—one, two, three.

Play at **/ = 100,** which means the tempo is 100 beats per minute (see APPENDIX IV).

$\frac{3}{4}$ **G**   **D**   **G**   **D**

/ / /   / / /   / / /   ◇.

D G B   D F# A   *(repeat the line)*

◇. = play once and hold the chord for 3 beats

THE A MAJOR CHORD

A Major (first inversion)

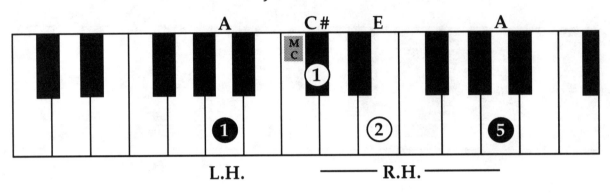

Play A Major in arpeggio style—C#, E, A, E—one note of the chord for each diagonal line.

With the *first finger* of the *left hand* play the bass note (**A**) in the octave below middle C.

$\frac{4}{4}$ **A**

/ / / /   / / / /   / / / /   / / / /

C# E A E

Play D, G, and A in arpeggio style—one note for each beat.

/ = 140

$\frac{4}{4}$ **D**   **G**   **A**   **A**

/ / / /   / / / /   / / / /   / / / / :||

(repeat the line)

EXERCISE 5

Play in arpeggio style, one note of the chord for each beat.

♩ = 112

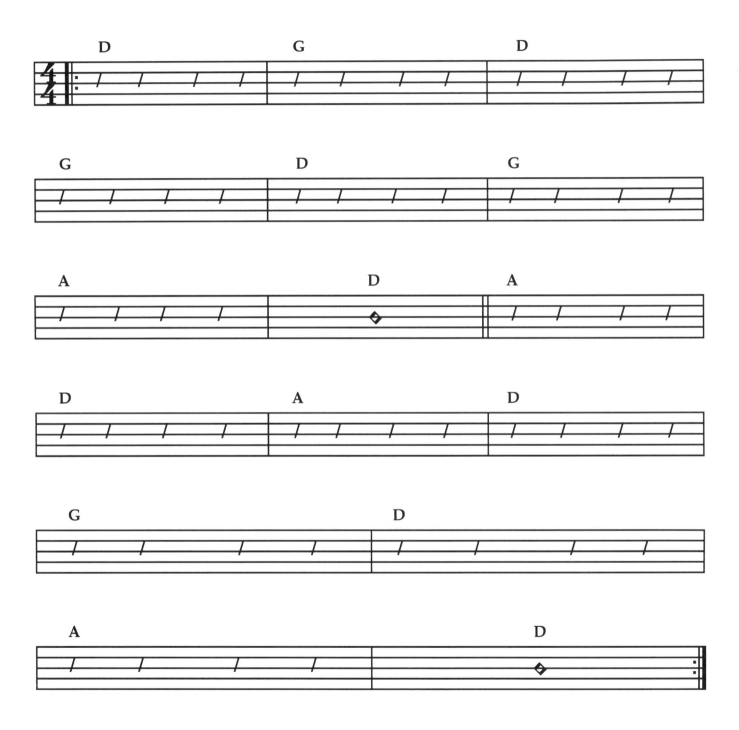

EXERCISE 6

Play, chording one, two, three, four (no arpeggios).

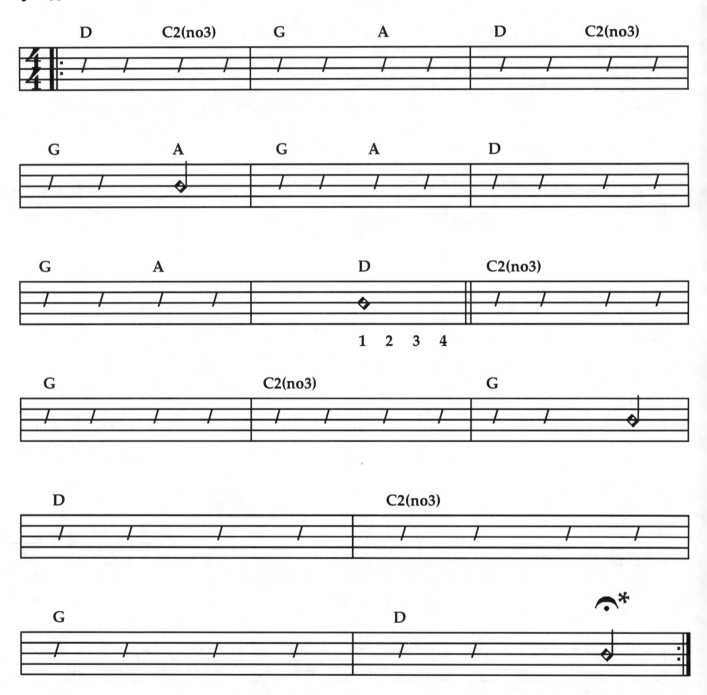

*⌢• = play once and hold the chord extra long

THANK YOU AGAIN–Key of D

♩ = 78

Sandy Hoffman

CHORUS:

Lord, I want to say — thank You a - gain — thank You for lov-

— ing me Lord, I want to say — thank You a - gain-

— for sav - ing my soul— Lord, I can't re - pay-

— all that You gave —, all that You gave — for me

Lord, here in my heart — thank You a - gain— for sav - ing my soul-

(REST)

— Thank You a - gain — for sav - ing my soul —

THEY'RE FOR YOU–Key of D

Sandy Hoffman

V. THE KEY OF E MAJOR

CHORDS IN THE KEY OF E

Key of E **CHORD NAME:**	E	F#m	G#m	A	B	C#m	D#dim	E
SCALE DEGREE NUMBER:	I	ii	iii	**IV**	V	vi	vii	I

E Major–root position (built upon scale degree I)

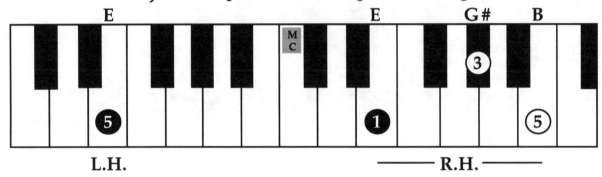

A2(no3)[1]–second inversion (built upon scale degree IV)

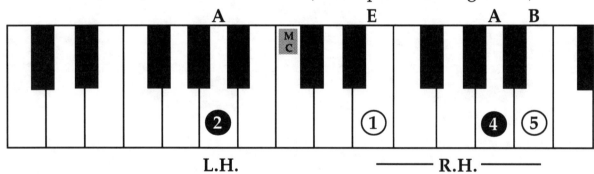

Bsus–first inversion (built upon scale degree V)

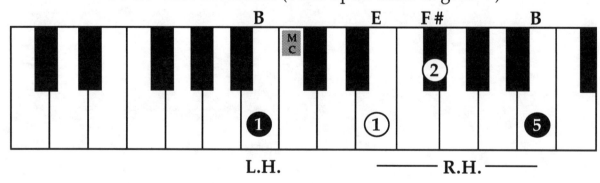

[1] See page 28, ABOUT COLOR CHORDS

ABOUT KEYBOARD PADS

I.   *Pads* are often played on the electronic keyboard. These notes or chords are held for longer numbers of beats and mimic the sounds of stringed instruments, string orchestras, electronic organs, and other legato instruments.

II.   In the ensemble setting, pads fill sonic holes left by rhythmic instruments. Use them sparingly (less is more) and they will add warmth and fullness to the sound of the band.

III. To pad a chord, play all or part of the chord on the first beat of the measure and hold the keys down for the remaining three beats. *This is called a "whole note rhythm" pattern.*

To pad the E Major chord[1], play as follows:

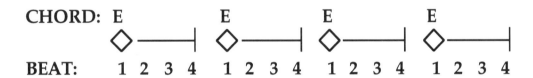

```
CHORD:  E             E             E             E
        ◇———┤  ◇———┤  ◇———┤  ◇———┤
BEAT:   1 2 3 4   1 2 3 4   1 2 3 4   1 2 3 4
```

Remember to play the bass note of the E Major chord (**E**) with the *fifth finger* of the *left hand* on the first beat of each new measure.

IV.   The keyboardist may also play two pads per measure–one pad for each two beats. *This is called a "half note rhythm" pattern.*

```
CHORD:  E             E             E             E
        ♦┤♦┤  ♦┤♦┤  ♦┤♦┤  ♦┤♦┤
BEAT:   1 2 3 4   1 2 3 4   1 2 3 4   1 2 3 4
```

---
[1] See page 48, CHORDS IN THE KEY OF E

THE E MAJOR CHORD

E Major (root position)

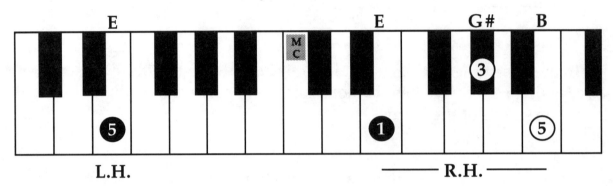

Play E Major in pad style *(whole note rhythm)*. **Chord on the first beat of each measure and hold the keys down for the remaining three beats.**

With the *fifth finger* of the *left hand* play the bass note (**E**) in the octave below middle C.

$\frac{4}{4}$ E ◇   1 2 3 4   E ◇   1 2 3 4   E ◇   1 2 3 4   E ◇   1 2 3 4

Play E Major in pad style *(half note rhythm)*. **Chord on the first and third beat of each measure and hold the keys down for the second and fourth beat.**

$\frac{4}{4}$ E ◇ 1   ♩ 2   ◇ 3   ♩ 4 | E ◇ 1   ♩ 2   ◇ 3   ♩ 4 | E ◇ 1   ♩ 2   ◇ 3   ♩ 4 | E ◇ 1   ♩ 2   ◇ 3   ♩ 4 :||

THE A2(no3) CHORD

A2(no3) (second inversion)

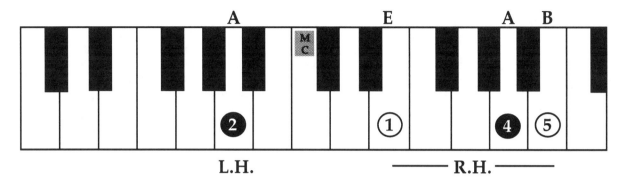

L.H.   ———— R.H. ————

Play A2(no3) in pad style. Chord on the first beat of each measure and hold the keys down for the remaining two beats. *This is called a "dotted half note rhythm" pattern.*

With the *second finger* of the *left hand* play the bass note (**A**) in the octave below middle C.

♩ = 108

3/4   **A2(no3)**
        ◇• 2-3   ◇• 2-3   ◇• 2-3   ◇• 2-3
        1

Play A2(no3) and E Major in pad style *(dotted half note rhythm).*

♩ = 160

3/4   **A2(no3)**   **E**   **A2(no3)**
        ◇• 2-3   ◇• 2-3   ◇• 2-3   ◇• 2-3 :‖
        1

THE Bsus CHORD

Bsus (first inversion)

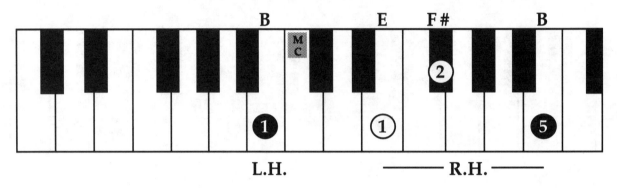

Play Bsus in pad style *(half note and whole note rhythms).*

With the *first finger* of the *left hand* play the bass note (**B**) in the octave below middle C.

♩ = 92

Play Bsus, A2(no3), and E Major in pad style *(half note and whole note rhythms).*

♩ = 72

EXERCISE 7

Play A2(no3), Bsus, and E in pad style *(half note and whole note rhythms).*

♩ = 80

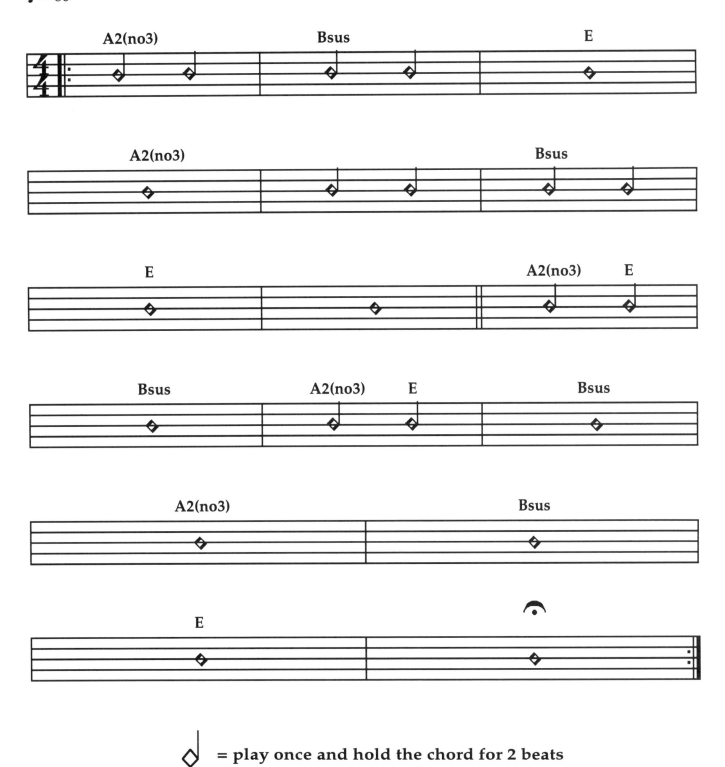

♦♩ = play once and hold the chord for 2 beats

♦ = play once and hold the chord for 4 beats

EXERCISE 8

Play Bsus, A2(no3), and E in pad style *(dotted half note rhythm).*

♩ = 160

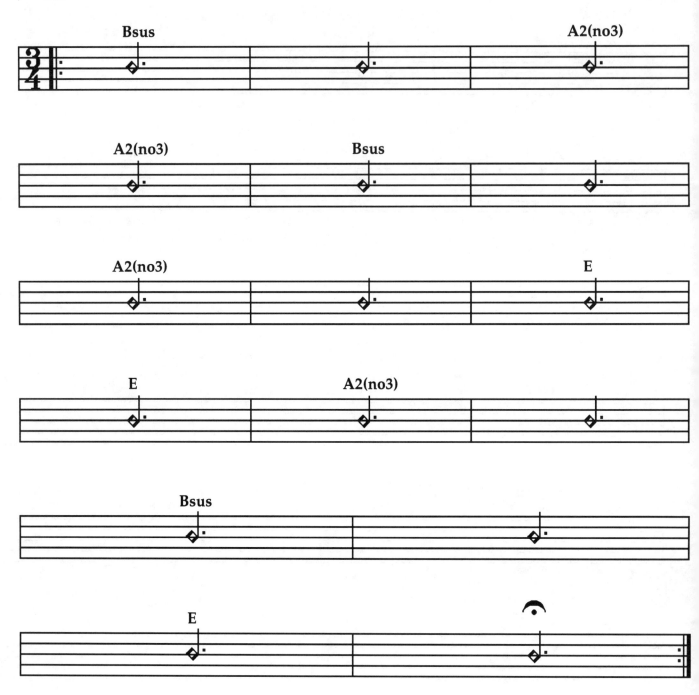

♢• = play once and hold the chord for 3 beats

THANK YOU AGAIN–Key of E

Sandy Hoffman

THEY'RE FOR YOU–Key of E

♩ = 76

Sandy Hoffman

VI. MINOR KEYS

ABOUT THE KEY OF A MINOR

I.   Each major key has a relative minor key. This means that they are kin to each other because they share a "key signature." They both have the same number of sharps and flats (see page 12).

II. To determine the relative minor key of any major key, simply step backwards down the musical alphabet one and one-half steps: C Major - B - B♭ - A Minor.

This backward movement down the musical alphabet takes us *from the key of C Major to the key of A Minor.*

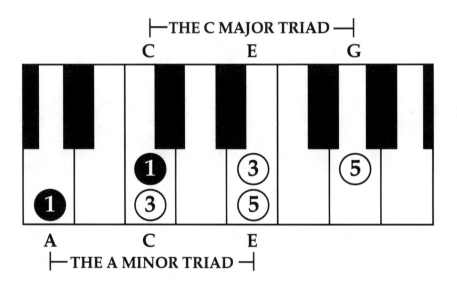

III. The key of A Minor is relative to the key of C Major. They both have *no* sharps or flats.

CHORDS IN THE KEY OF A MINOR

Key of Am **CHORD NAME**:	**Am**	Bm	C	**Dm**	E	F	G	**Am**
SCALE DEGREE NUMBER:	**i**	ii	III	**iv**	**V**	VI	VII	**i**

Am–root position (built upon scale degree i)

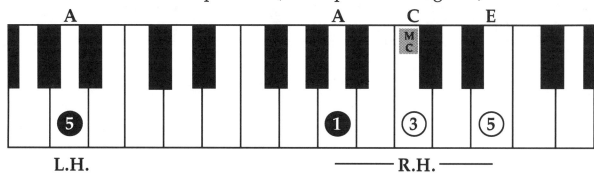

Dm–second inversion (built upon scale degree iv)

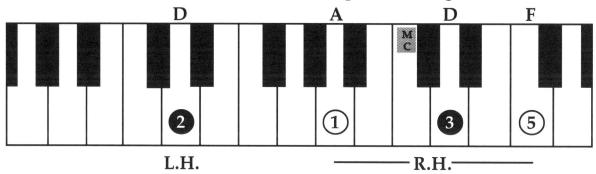

E Major–first inversion (built upon scale degree V)

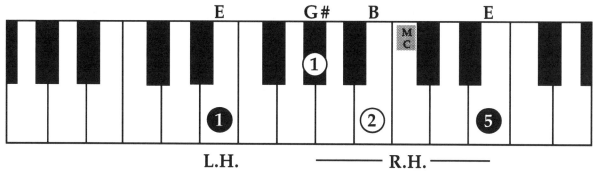

THE A Minor CHORD

Am (root position)

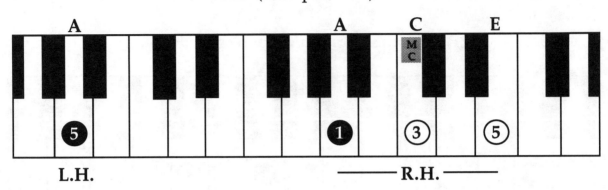

Play A minor, chording steadily one, two, three, four.

With the *fifth finger* of the *left hand* play the bass note (**A**) in the second octave below middle C. Do this on the first beat of each measure.

/ = 112

4/4 Am   Am   Am   Am
     / / / /   / / / /   / / / /   / / / /

Play A minor in pad style *(whole note rhythm)*.

/ = 60

4/4 A m   A m   A m   A m
     ◇   ◇   ◇   ◇

THE D Minor CHORD

Dm (second inversion)

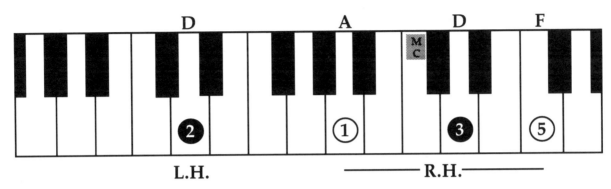

L.H. ——————— R.H.———

Play D minor, chording steadily one, two, three.

With the *second finger* of the *left hand* play the bass note (**D**) in the octave below middle C.

/ = 112

$\frac{3}{4}$ Dm   Dm   D m   D m
     / / /   / / /   / / /   ◊.   :‖

(repeat the line)

Pad Dm, Am, and E *(dotted half note rhythm)*.

/ = 112

$\frac{3}{4}$ D m   Am   E   A m
     ◊· 2-3   ◊· 2-3   ◊· 2-3   ◊· 2-3 :‖

EXERCISE 9

Play, chording steadily one, two, three, four.

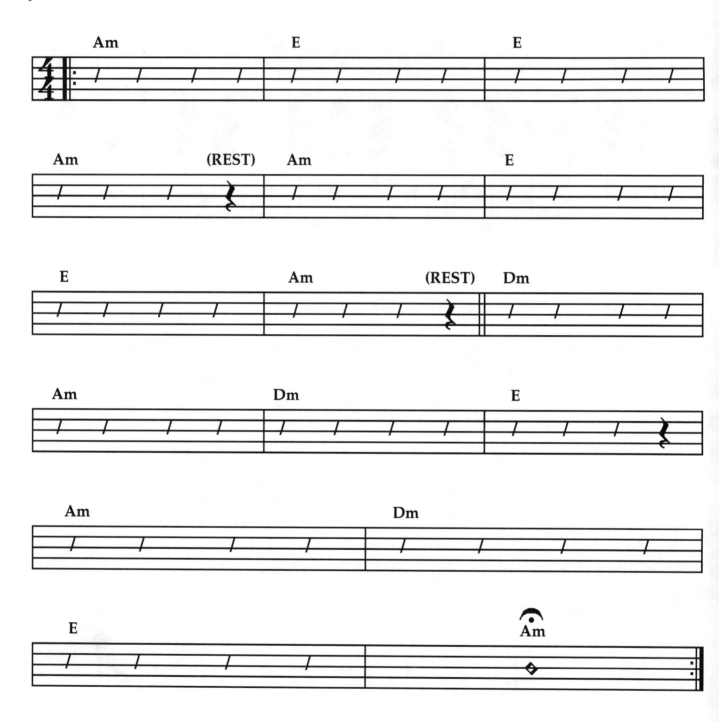

ABOUT THE KEY OF E MINOR

REMEMBER:

I. Each major key has a relative minor key. This means that they are kin to each other because they share a key signature. They both have the same number of sharps and flats (see page 12).

II. To determine the relative minor key of a major, simply step backwards down the musical alphabet one and one-half steps: G - G♭ - F - E.

This backward movement down the musical alphabet takes us *from the key of G Major to the key of E Minor.*

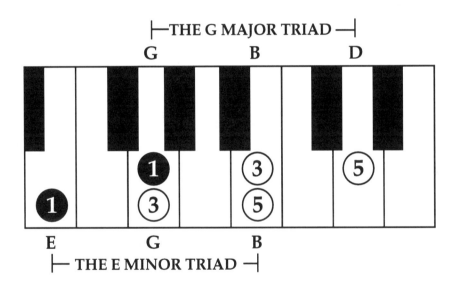

III. The key of E Minor is relative to the key of G Major. They both have *one* sharp.

CHORDS IN THE KEY OF E MINOR

Key of Em **CHORD NAME:**	**Em**	F#m	G	**Am**	**B**	C	D	**Em**
SCALE DEGREE NUMBER:	**i**	ii	III	**iv**	**V**	VI	VII	**i**

Em–root position (built upon scale degree i)

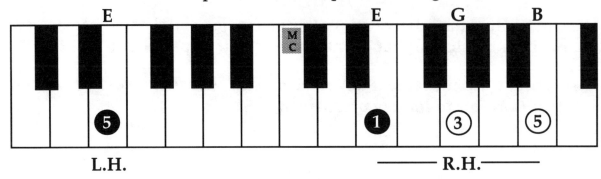

Am–second inversion (built upon scale degree iv)

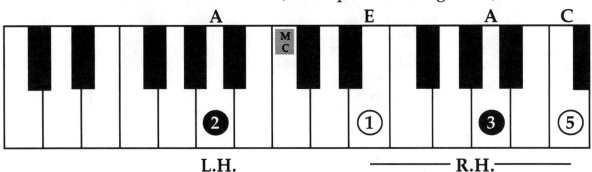

Bsus–first inversion (built upon scale degree V)

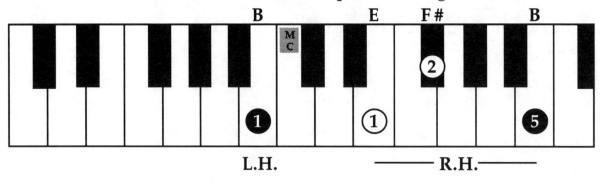

THE E Minor CHORD

Em (root position)

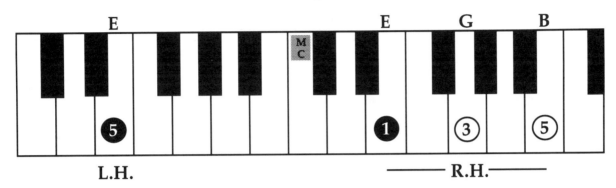

Play E minor, chording steadily one, two, three, four.

With the *fifth finger* of the *left hand* play the bass note (E) in the octave below middle C.

/ = 96

$\frac{4}{4}$ Em   Em   Em   Em
     / / / /   / / / /   / / / /   / / / /

Play E minor, A minor, and Bsus.

/ = 88

$\frac{4}{4}$ E m   Am   Bsus   Em
     / / / /   ◇   / / / /   ◇   :‖

A SENSE OF PLACE

♩ = 72

Sandy Hoffman

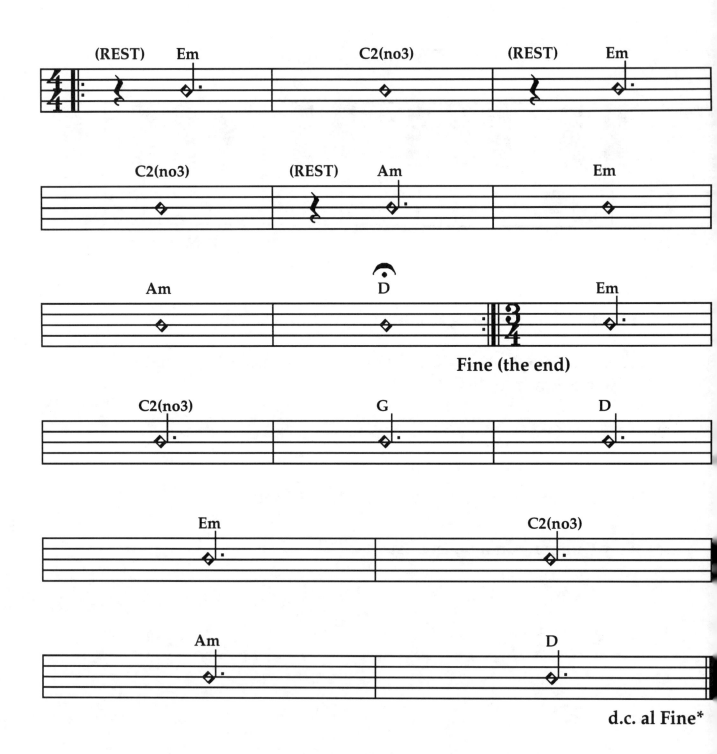

Fine (the end)

d.c. al Fine*

* **d.c. al Fine** = go back to the beginning and play until you reach **Fine (the end)**

VII. ALL TOGETHER NOW!

CHORDS FOR:

CLEAN HANDS AND A PURE HEART

D (root position)

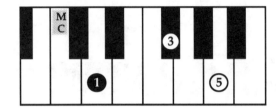

G (second inversion)

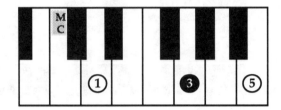

A (first inversion)

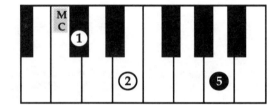

E (root position)

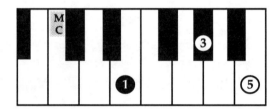

Em (root position)

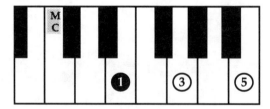

CLEAN HANDS AND A PURE HEART

Play, chording 1, 2, 3, 4 or / / / /.

♩ = 92

Sandy Hoffman

CHORUS

Clean hands- and a pure — heart — lead me, Lord —, in - to —

— Your- pres — ence- Clean hands- and a pure — heart — the

on - ly path — in - to — Your- hol - i- ness — I con -fess-

clean — hands and a pure — pure heart –

clean — hands and a pure-

— pure heart —

CHORDS FOR:

FULFILL OUR LONGING

E (root position)

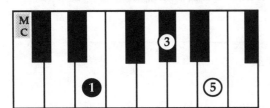

A2(no3) (second inversion)

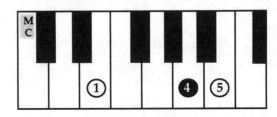

Bsus (first inversion)

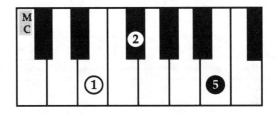

A NEW CHORD:

C#m7 (root position)

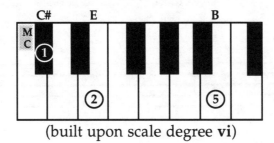

(built upon scale degree **vi**)

Play the bass note (**C#**) with the *fifth finger* of the *left hand*.

FULFILL OUR LONGING

Play, arpeggiating twice per measure.

Sandy Hoffman

♩ = 77

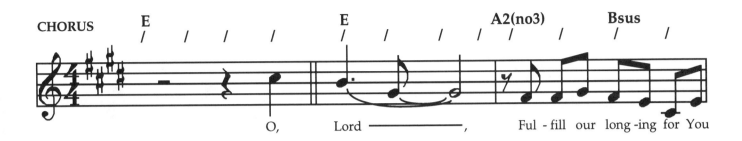

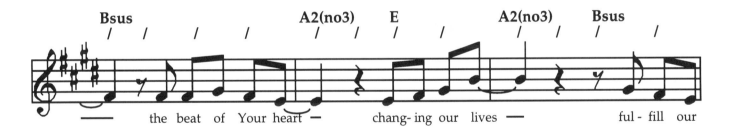

CHORDS FOR:
TAKE ME THERE

G (root position)

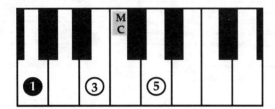

C2(no3) (second inversion)

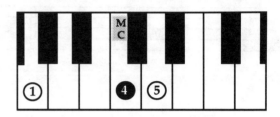

A NEW CHORD:

A7 (second inversion)

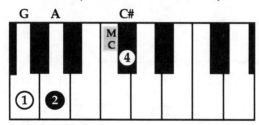

(built upon scale degree **V of V**)

Play the bass note (**A**) with the *fourth finger* of the *left hand.*

TAKE ME THERE
Play, using keyboard pads.

Sandy Hoffman

YOUR NOTES:

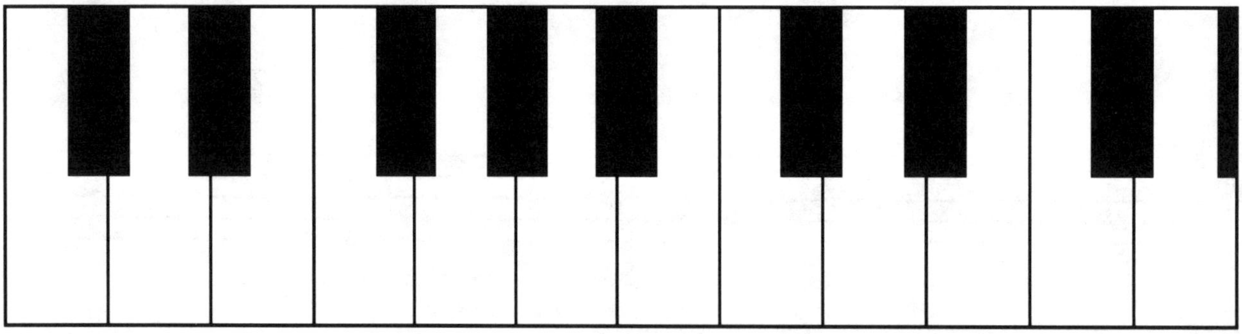

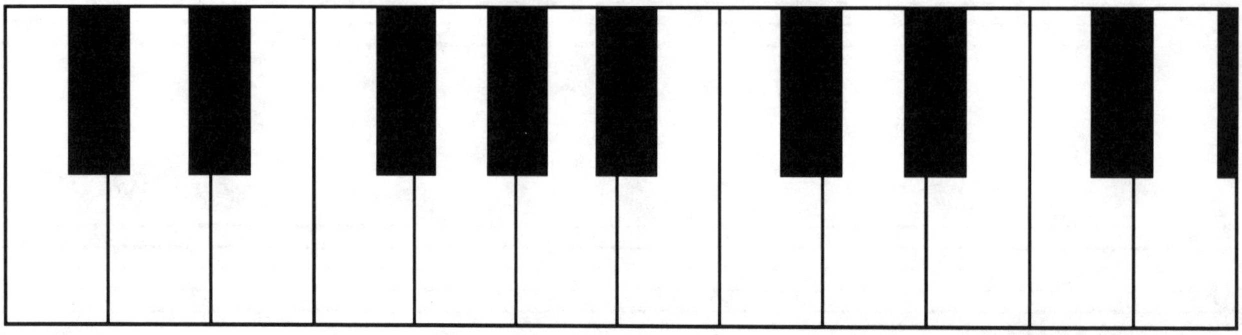

_____

_____

_____

_____

_____

_____

_____

_____

APPENDICES

THE NUMBER SYSTEM

The Number System is a system which is used to communicate and cross reference chord progressions.

I.   **A chord progression is a series of chords played in a predetermined sequence.**

Chord:	C	F	G	C	C	F	G	C
Beat Number:	**1,2**	**3,4**	**1,2**	**3,4**	**1,2**	**3,4**	**1,2**	**3,4**

II.   **In addition to calling chords by their letter names, C, F, G, and so on, chords can be identified by numbers. For instance, in the key of C, the C chord is chord number I. Starting with C and counting four up the scale to F makes F the number IV chord and G the number V chord.**

Chord:	C	Dm	Em	F	G	Am	Bdim.	C
Chord Number:	I	ii	iii	IV	V	vi	vii	I

III.   **Now instead of calling it the "C, F, G" chord progression we can identify it as the "I, IV, V" chord progression.**

Chord:	C	F	G	C	C	F	G	C
Chord Number:	I	IV	V	I	I	IV	V	I
Beat Number:	**1,2**	**3,4**	**1,2**	**3,4**	**1,2**	**3,4**	**1,2**	**3,4**

IV.   **It is easy to recognize the benefit of communicating with the number system. If we use numbers instead of letters to indicate chord progressions, we are then free to use the same chord progression in as many different keys as we like without ever having to rewrite the music.**

Number:	I	IV	V	I		I	IV	V	I
Chord:	C	F	G	C		C	F	G	C
	G	C	D	G		G	C	D	G
	D	G	A	D		D	G	A	D
	E	A	B	E		E	A	B	E

THE KEYS

The Circle of 5ths: There is an interval of a fifth (3 1/2 steps) between each of the following keys. Using the circle of 5ths (beginning with the key of C) will help you to remember the key names and number of sharps or flats in each.

key of C to key of G:	C	D	E	F	G
count up the scale:	1	2	3	4	5

KEY	NUMBER OF SHARPS (#) or FLATS (♭)	
C	0 sharps or flats	
G	1 sharp	(F#)
D	2 sharps	(F#, C#)
A	3 sharps	(F#, C#, G#)
E	4 sharps	(F#, C#, G#, D#)
B (C♭—7 flats)	5 sharps	(F#, C#, G#, D#, A#)
F# (G♭—6 flats)	6 sharps	(F#, C#, G#, D#, A#, E#)
C# (D♭—5 flats)	7 sharps	(F#, C#, G#, D#, A#, E#, B#)
A♭	4 flats	(B♭, E♭, A♭, D♭)
E♭	3 flats	(B♭, E♭, A♭)
B♭	2 flats	(B♭, E♭)
F	1 flat	(B♭)

TUNING THE BAND

The job of tuning the band often falls to the worship keyboardist. The following diagrams show the names of the strings of the guitar, bass guitar, and violin and where they are located on the keyboard.

The guitar is most commonly an instrument of six strings. They are numbered from the lowest to the highest, 6 - 5 - 4 - 3 - 2 - 1. Their letter names are E - A - D - G - B - E. The lowest note of the guitar, E, is located in the octave below middle C.

TUNING THE GUITAR

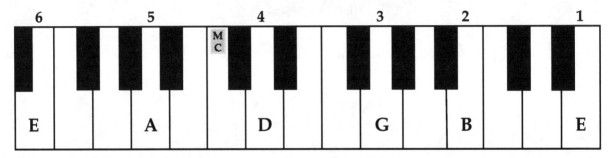

TUNING THE BASS GUITAR

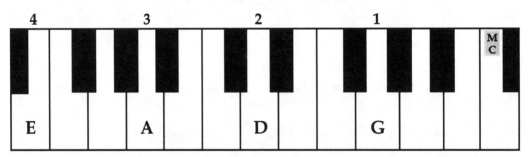

TUNING THE VIOLIN

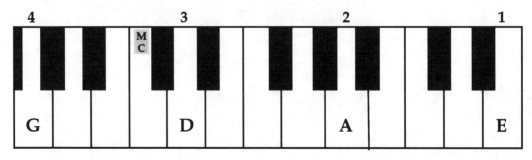

THE METRONOME
(tempo markings)

I.   **THE METRONOME** is a device (mechanical or electronic) which clicks in perfect, steady time and allows the musician to practice without missing a beat. Tempo markings or "metronome settings" will be expressed as:

note = number of beats   *or*   slash = number of beats

$$\quad = 100 \qquad\qquad / = 100$$

II.   The note or the slash represents one beat. The number (from 0 to 200) represents the number of beats per minute.

/ = **100** means that the speed of the song or exercise is 100 beats per minute. Simply set your metronome to 100 and it will click 100 steady times per minute. This will give you a reference for developing a sense of consistent rhythm on your instrument.

IN CLOSING

Mission Statement
The mission of Worship Works! Music is to honor and glorify God with contemporary praise and worship by reaching out to the unsaved and leading the saved into the presence of the Almighty.

Foundational Scripture
"For we are His workmanship, created in Christ Jesus for good works, which God prepared beforehand that we should walk in them."
                                        Ephesians 2:10

Questions?

E-mail: *sandy@essentialworship.com*
Website: *www.essentialworship.com*

"because worship is essential"